Did You Say Pears?

Arlene Alda

Tundra Books

Published in Canada by Tundra Books,
481 University Avenue, Toronto, Ontario M5G 2E9

Published in the United States by Tundra Books of Northern New York,
P.O. Box 1030, Plattsburgh, New York 12901

Library of Congress Control Number: 2005901424

Library and Archives Canada Cataloguing in Publication

Alda, Arlene, 1933-
      Did you say pears? / Arlene Alda.

ISBN 0-88776-739-7

      1. English language—Homonyms—Juvenile literature.
2. Homonyms—Juvenile literature. I. Title.

PZ8.3.A42Di 2006   j428.1   C2005-901105-X

We acknowledge the financial support of the Government of Canada through
the Book Publishing Industry Development Program (BPIDP) and that of the Government
of Ontario through the Ontario Media Development Corporation's Ontario Book
Initiative. We further acknowledge the support of the Canada Council for the
Arts and the Ontario Arts Council for our publishing program.

ONTARIO ARTS COUNCIL
CONSEIL DES ARTS DE L'ONTARIO

Printed in Hong Kong, China

1 2 3 4 5 6   11 10 09 08 07 06

Dedicated to Izzy, with deep love and thanks
for being so incredibly eager and helpful.

If horns

played cool music

And pants

were just clothes . . .

If nails

were on fingers

And a
trunk

were a
nose...

If a pitcher

could
pour

And glasses

could see . . .

If waves

could have hands, like you and like me . . .

If all peas

were letters

And blew

were the sky . . .

If rows

could be fragrant

And
flower

made pie . . .

If the sun

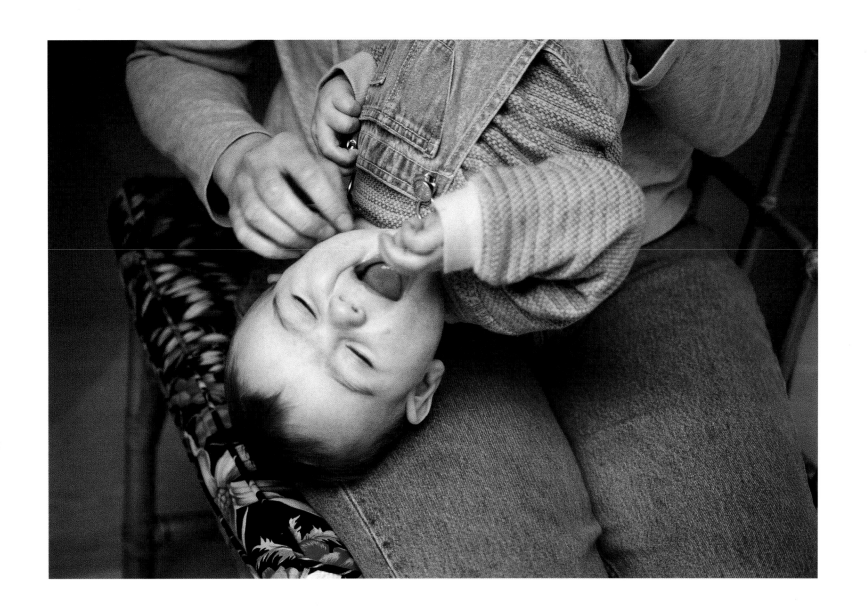

could laugh

And
stairs

were blank stares . . .

Don't you agree that pairs

could be pears?

WORDS, WORDS . . .

Homonyms are words that sound alike,
have the same spelling,
but have different meanings.

4, 5	horns, horns
6, 7	pants, pants
8, 9	nails, nails
10, 11	trunk, trunk
12, 13	pitcher, pitcher
14, 15	glasses, glasses
16, 17	waves, waves

Homophones are words that sound alike,
but have different spellings,
and different meanings.

18, 19	peas, Pp's
20, 21	blew, blue
22, 23	rows, rose
24, 25	flower, flour
26, 27	sun, son
28, 29	stairs, stares
30, 31	pairs, pears